STEM

3-D PRINTING

Adding and Subtracting Fractions

Molly Bibbo, M.A.T.

Consultants

Michele Ogden, Ed.D
Principal
Irvine Unified School District

Colleen Pollitt, M.A.Ed.
Math Support Teacher
Howard County Public Schools

Publishing Credits

Rachelle Cracchiolo, M.S.Ed., *Publisher*
Conni Medina, M.A.Ed., *Managing Editor*
Dona Herweck Rice, *Series Developer*
Emily R. Smith, M.A.Ed., *Series Developer*
Diana Kenney, M.A.Ed., NBCT, *Content Director*
Stacy Monsman, M.A., *Editor*
Kevin Panter, *Graphic Designer*

Image Credits: pp.4–5 laboratory/Alamy Stock Photo; p.8 Wu Kailiang/Alamy Stock Photo; p.9 Sergio Azenha/Alamy Stock Photo; pp.10–11 Piero Cruciatti/Alamy Stock Photo; p.10 (top) MBI/Alamy Stock Photo; p.11 (bottom) Josef Kubes/Alamy Stock Photo; pp.12, 13 Brian Snyder/Reuters; p.14 Photo by Frankie Flood; pp.16, 16–17 BSIP/UIG via Getty Images; pp.20–21 STR/AFP/Getty Images; p.21 (top) VCG/VCG via Getty Images, (bottom) HAP/Quirky China News/REX/Shutterstock; pp.22 (top and bottom), 23 (bottom) VCG/VCG via Getty Images; pp.24–25 Laurie Rubin/Getty Images; p.26 (bottom) Piero Cruciatti/Alamy Stock Photo; p.27 (top) Phanie/Alamy Stock Photo; pp.26–27 Patti McConville/Alamy Stock Photo; p.29 Courtesy of Team UnLimbited; p.31 ZUMA Press, Inc./Alamy Stock Photo; all other images from iStock and/or Shutterstock.

Library of Congress Cataloging-in-Publication Data

Names: Bibbo, Molly Suzanne, author.
Title: STEM. 3-D printing / Molly Suzanne Bibbo, M.A.T.
Other titles: 3-D printing
Description: Huntington Beach, CA : Teacher Created Materials, [2018] | Audience: Grades 4-6. | Includes index.
Identifiers: LCCN 2017011902 (print) | LCCN 2017039604 (ebook) | ISBN 9781480759367 (eBook) | ISBN 9781425855543 (pbk.)
Subjects: LCSH: Tissue engineering--Juvenile literature. | Three-dimensional printing--Juvenile literature. | Fractions--Juvenile literature.
Classification: LCC R857.T55 (ebook) | LCC R857.T55 B53 2018 (print) | DDC 610.28/4--dc23
LC record available at https://lccn.loc.gov/2017011902

Teacher Created Materials
5301 Oceanus Drive
Huntington Beach, CA 92649-1030
http://www.tcmpub.com

ISBN 978-1-4258-5554-3

Printed by 51250
PO51463 / Printed in USA

Table of Contents

A New World of Printing

Imagine being able to design your very own toy on a computer. Next, imagine being able to print that toy on a printer. It turns out, that's not too far out of reach!

Technology is changing the way we live. It has changed how we communicate. It has changed the way we travel. It has changed the way we learn. It has given people a better quality of life. Doctors and scientists are using technology to help people in need. In some cases, it is helping to save people's lives.

A 3-D printer produces a small spaceman.

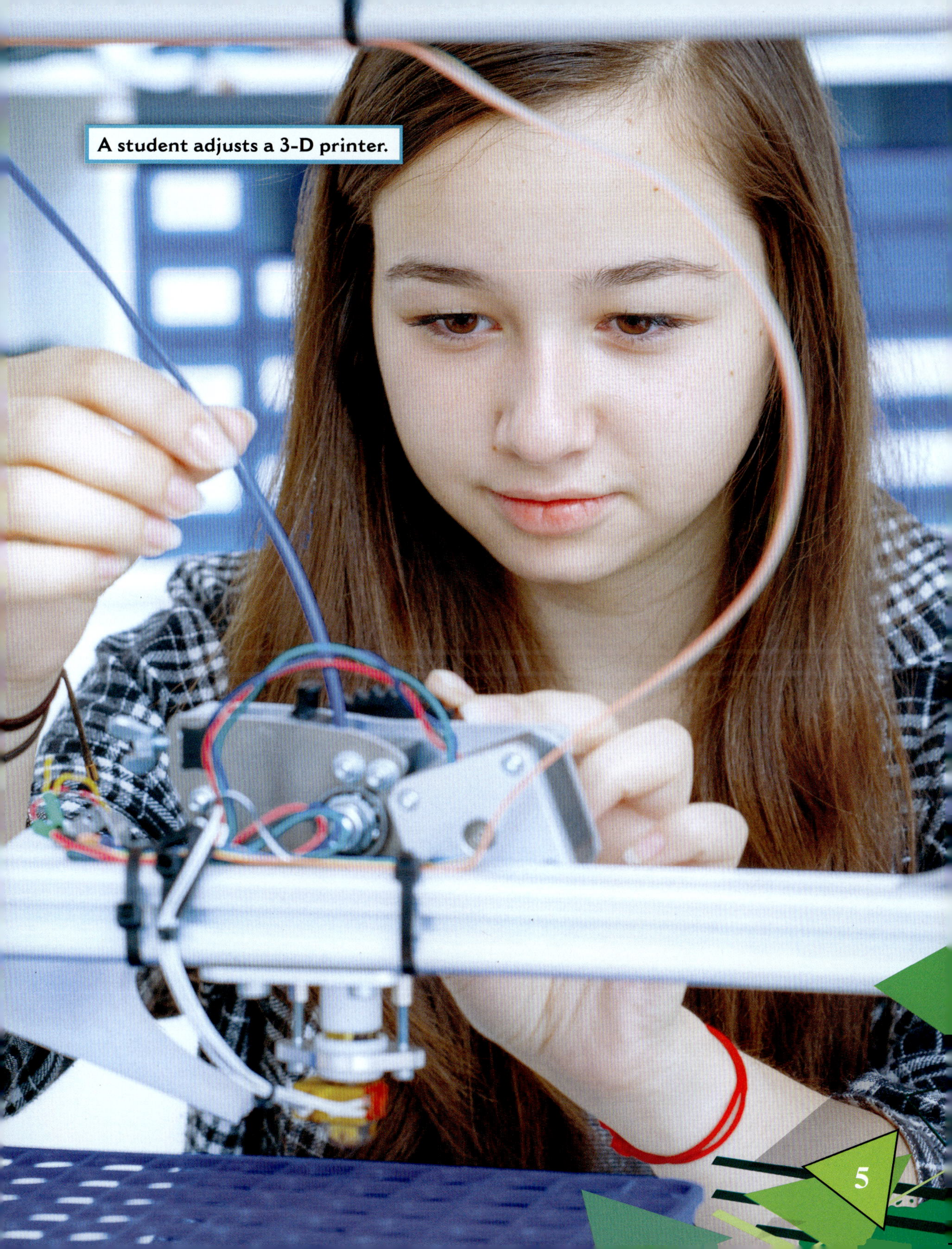

A student adjusts a 3-D printer.

Imagine dipping your hand in paint to create a handprint on a sheet of paper. When you look at your handprint, you see that the mark of your hand is flat. Flat objects are 2-D, or **2-dimensional**. Shapes like squares, triangles, and circles are 2-D.

However, not all shapes and objects are 2-dimensional. Your physical hand is thicker than a sheet of paper. Your hand is 3-D, or **3-dimensional**. In fact, your whole body is 3-D. Objects that are 3-D have thickness, or **depth**. A cube or a sphere is 3-D. A cardboard box or a rubber ball is 3-D. Take a look around you—almost all of the everyday items you use are 3-D.

LET'S EXPLORE MATH

Monica is printing birthday party invitations. She prints $\frac{2}{6}$ of the invitations on Monday. She prints $\frac{3}{6}$ of the invitations on Wednesday.

1. How can $\frac{2}{6}$ be decomposed into unit fractions? Draw a model to show your thinking.
2. What fraction of the invitations does Monica print on Monday and Wednesday? Write an equation to show your solution.
3. What fraction of the invitations does Monica still need to print? Explain your reasoning.

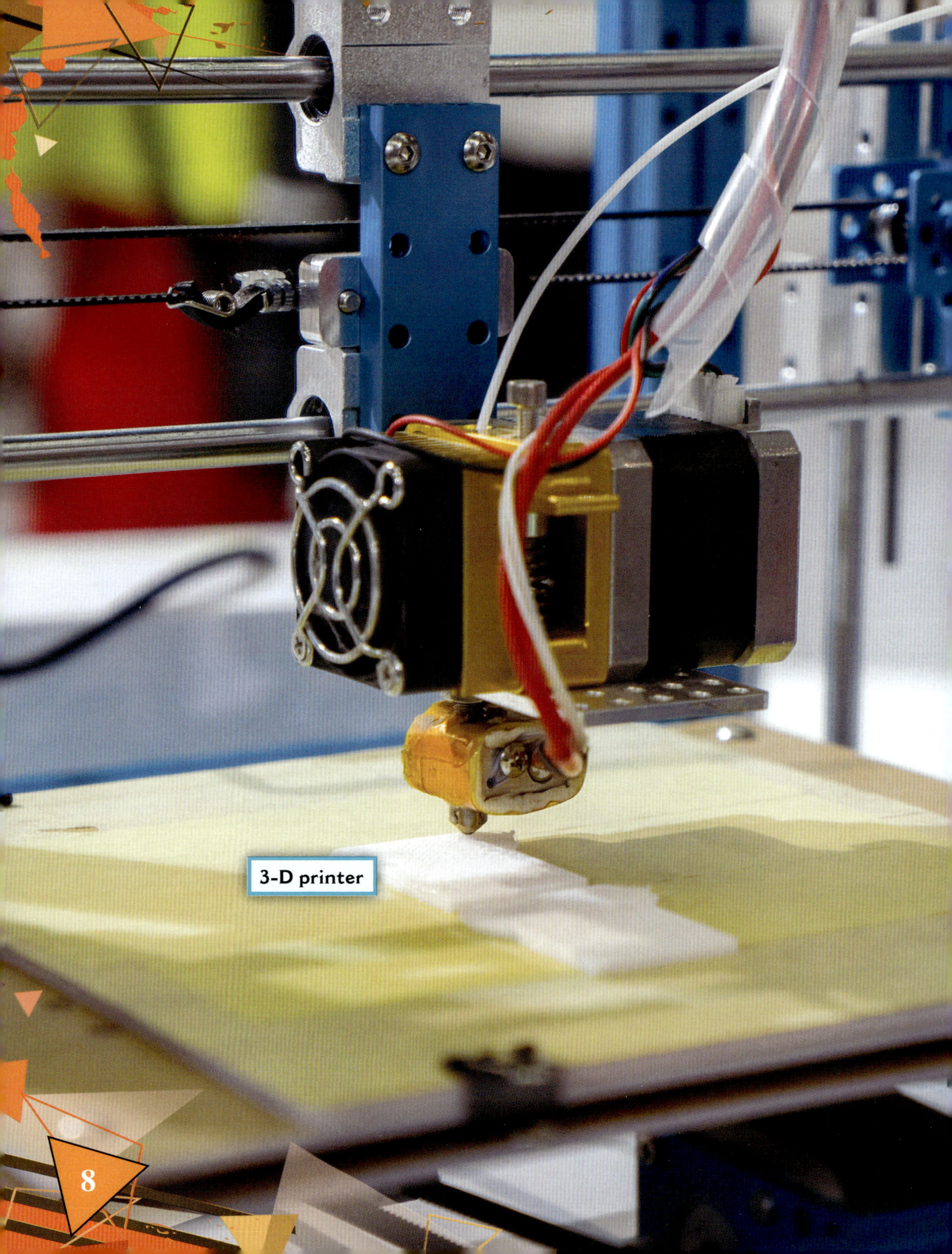
3-D printer

3-D Printing

Wouldn't it be cool to be able to print a piece of chocolate whenever you wanted one? With a 3-D printer, you can do just that! But, how does it work? A 3-D printer prints layers on top of layers to give an object depth. The idea is similar to building a tower with blocks. At first, you create one row with blocks. Then, you stack another row of blocks on top. As you add more layers of blocks, your tower gets taller. A 3-D printer works the same way.

A 3-D printer doesn't use liquid ink like a 2-D printer. Instead, it uses a solid material. This material is called **filament**. Some examples are plastic, metal, and (you guessed it) chocolate! Different types of filaments make different objects. Some 3-D printers print parts for cars and bikes. They use a metal filament called **titanium**. But, most 3-D printers use plastic filament. Plastic doesn't cost much, and it comes in a variety of colors.

plastic filament

An architect creates a 3–D model of a larger project.

How Does It Work?

The 3-D printing process isn't very complex. First, a computer uses a 3-D program to create a design of an object. The program slices the design into hundreds of thin, **horizontal** layers. It is then uploaded into a 3-D printer. The printer makes the object layer by layer. It melts plastic filament, which is then squeezed through a **nozzle**. The bottom layer is made first. Slowly, layers are added. Sometimes the layers are so thin you can't even see them! The computer sends messages to the printer about how to build each layer. This gives the object a certain shape. By printing layer upon layer, 3-D printers can make objects like water bottles, cell phone cases, and even toys.

LET'S EXPLORE MATH

Suppose a 3-D printer takes $2\frac{3}{4}$ minutes to print two layers of an object. The second layer takes $1\frac{1}{4}$ minutes.

1. Show two ways to decompose $2\frac{3}{4}$ into a sum of fractions. Draw models to show your thinking.
2. How long does it take to print the first layer of the object?

3-D-printed model cars

A 3-D printer prints the ball of a whistle.

Printing Prosthetics

A 3-D printer can be life-changing to a person with a missing **limb**. A limb is a body part that helps move or hold something. Legs and arms are limbs. People may be missing limbs for different reasons. Some people are born without them. Other people might lose them because of accidents or illnesses. People can buy **prosthetic** limbs. But, they need to be custom made. This makes prosthetics quite costly. The cost ranges from $5,000 to $50,000! Most people cannot afford to buy one.

Luckily, 3-D printers can help. These printers can create prosthetic limbs. Printing a prosthetic limb is much more affordable than buying one. It only costs about $50. And, it can be made much faster. It only takes one day. Now, more people are able to get the prosthetics they need.

A 3-D printer prints a new plastic finger for a prosthetic hand.

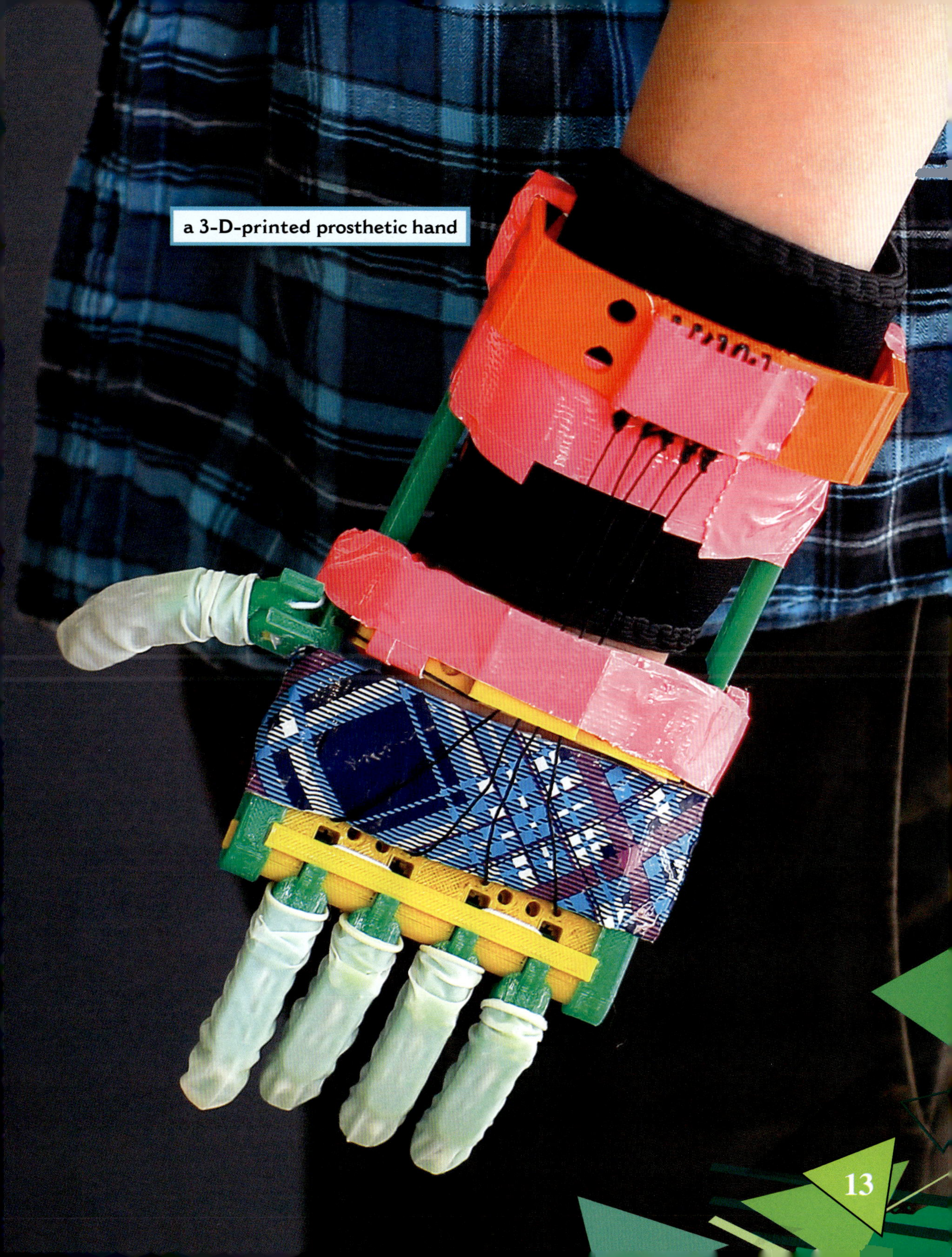

a 3-D-printed prosthetic hand

Stollenwerk picks up an object using her 3-D-printed prosthetic hand created by Professor Frankie Flood and his students at the University of Wisconsin-Milwaukee.

Shea's Hand

Shea Stollenwerk was born missing part of her right hand. When she was 8 years old, she asked for a new hand for Christmas. Her family knew a prosthetic hand could cost thousands of dollars. Thanks to a 3-D printer, she got her wish.

The first step in building Stollenwerk's prosthetic was to make a mold of her hand out of **plaster**. Plaster was poured to make a cast around the hand mold. Then, a computer took a 3-D **scan** of her hand. The 3-D printer built a hand that is just the right size for Stollenwerk. Her prosthetic hand can open and close. There are motors in the fingers that let her grab and hold things. Now, she can do many things she couldn't do before, like peel a banana, throw a ball, and play her viola.

LET'S EXPLORE MATH

Suppose a research team provides 3-D-printed hands to 12 kids in need. Of those kids, $\frac{8}{12}$ are boys. Choose all of the expressions that show the fraction of girls who get 3-D-printed hands.

A. $\frac{3}{12}$

B. $\frac{1}{12} + \frac{1}{12} + \frac{1}{12} + \frac{1}{12}$

C. $\frac{2}{12} + \frac{1}{12}$

D. $\frac{1}{12} + \frac{3}{12}$

Printing Tissue

While an arm or leg can be printed with plastic, some parts of the human body cannot. **Cells** are the building blocks of life. Human bodies are made out of millions of tiny cells. Cells grow and make new cells. New cells can only be made from other living cells. Cells come together to form **tissues**, which form all of our muscles and **organs**. Skin, hearts, and brains are all made of different kinds of tissues.

Luckily, some 3-D printers can do more than print plastic objects. Some printers can print cells. Some of them can even print actual, living tissue. They don't use plastic filament. Instead, they use living cells mixed with a special type of gel. The cells and gel work together to make new cells. All of the cells connect to make the kind of tissue needed. With this special 3-D printer, doctors can print the same tissue that makes organs.

image of 3-D-printed human tissue

A 3-D printer produces living tissue from layers of cells.

LET'S EXPLORE MATH

1. Suppose a 3-D printer prints a sample of cells that is $2\frac{1}{5}$ millimeters long. After 1 hour, the sample grows another $1\frac{4}{5}$ millimeters. How long is the sample now?
2. The sample needs to be 6 millimeters long. How many more millimeters does the sample need to grow?

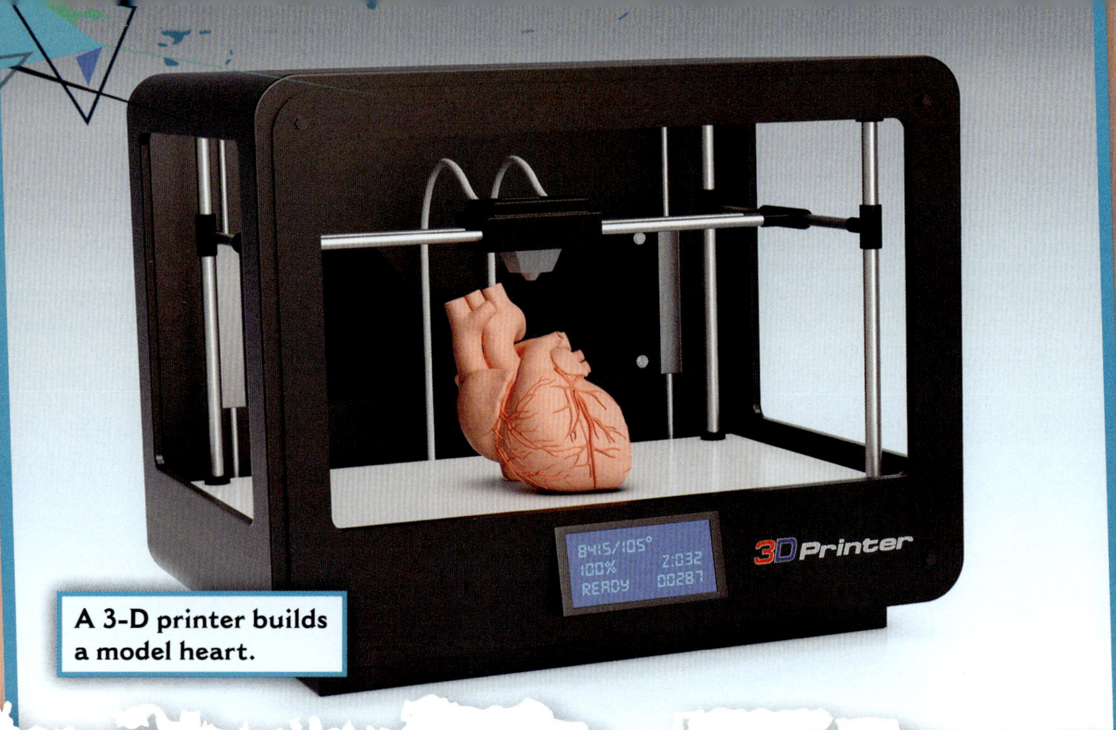

A 3-D printer builds a model heart.

A Printed Organ

Each organ in the human body has a unique job. Sometimes, an organ may be damaged. A person's heart or kidney may fail. Their liver may stop functioning. If the body cannot repair the damage, an organ **transplant** may be needed. These transplants only work when the new organ is an exact match for the person who needs it. Finding a perfect match is hard. Sometimes, doctors can't find the organs people need.

Scientists are working to find ways to get people what they need. One way is by developing a 3-D printer that can print organs. They want to go beyond printing tissue. They want to print organs that can be transplanted into people's bodies. Scientists are still working to make this happen. Until then, they are using 3-D printers to save people's lives in other ways.

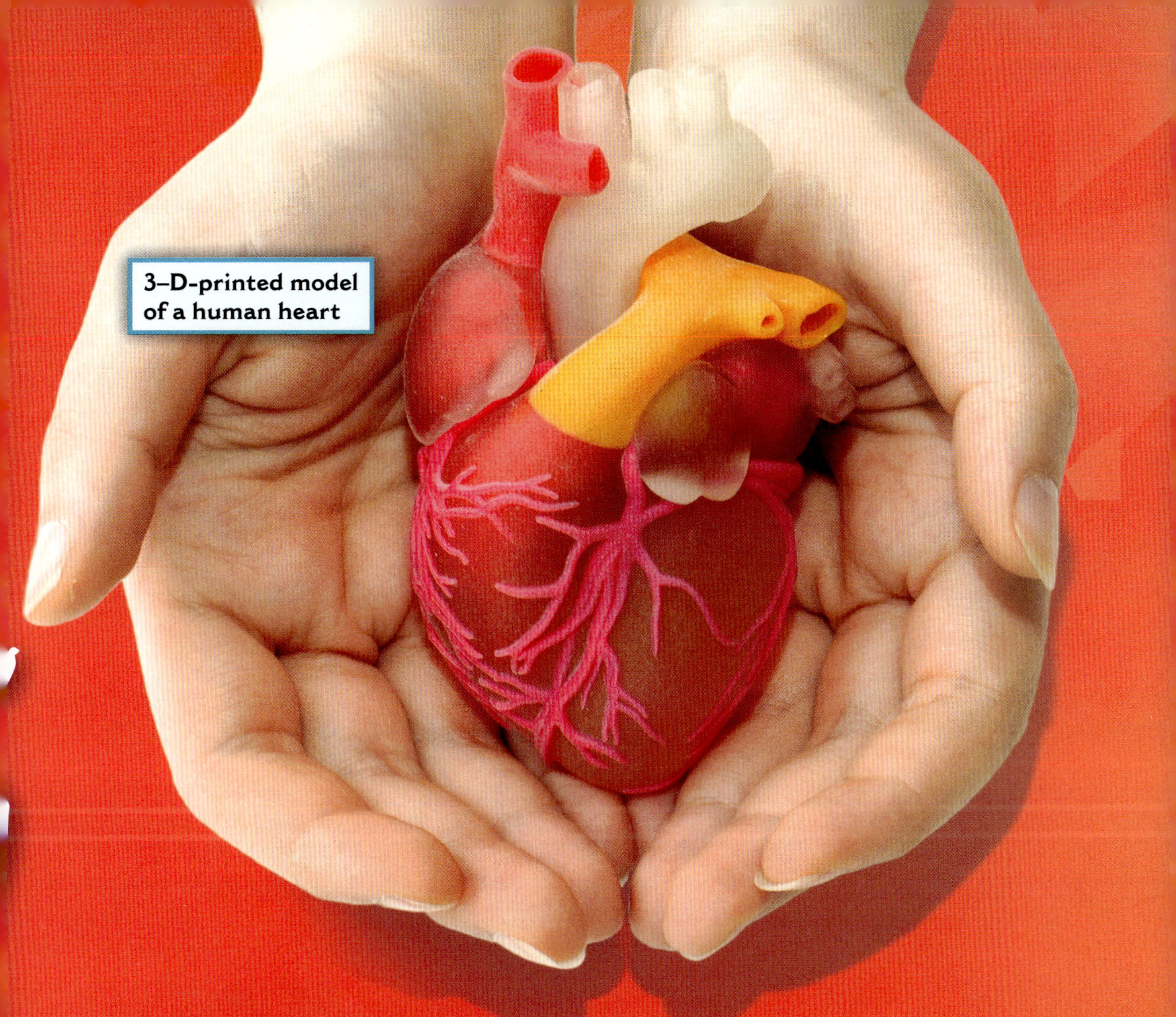

3-D-printed model of a human heart

LET'S EXPLORE MATH

The brain and the heart are two organs in a person's body. Choose all of the expressions that show combined brain and heart weights of less than 3 pounds.

A. $1\frac{3}{4} + 1\frac{3}{4}$

B. $1\frac{1}{2} + 1\frac{1}{2}$

C. $2\frac{1}{4} + \frac{1}{4}$

D. $1\frac{2}{6} + 2\frac{1}{6}$

Changing Lives

In October 2013, a man named Wei Hu fell three stories onto a pile of wood and crushed the left side of his skull. He survived, but part of his skull needed to be replaced. The accident damaged his brain and he was no longer able to speak or write. At first, doctors were not able to do much to help him. Then, they thought of 3-D printing.

Doctors use 3-D-printed titanium mesh to replace part of Hu's skull.

Doctors printed titanium mesh to replace part of Hu's skull. The metal is strong, so it will hold the shape of his skull and protect his brain. Once his brain heals, he will learn how to speak and write again.

Doctors believe that 3-D printers will one day be able to print metal bones to replace damaged ones. This could help many people.

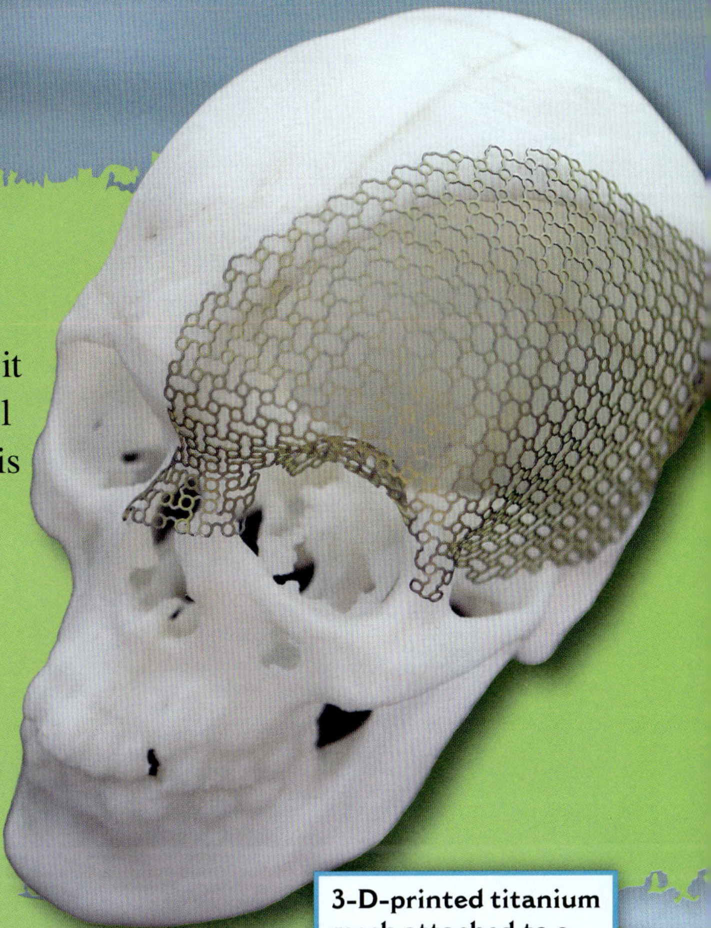

3-D-printed titanium mesh attached to a model of Hu's skull

Hu visits his doctor after his surgery.

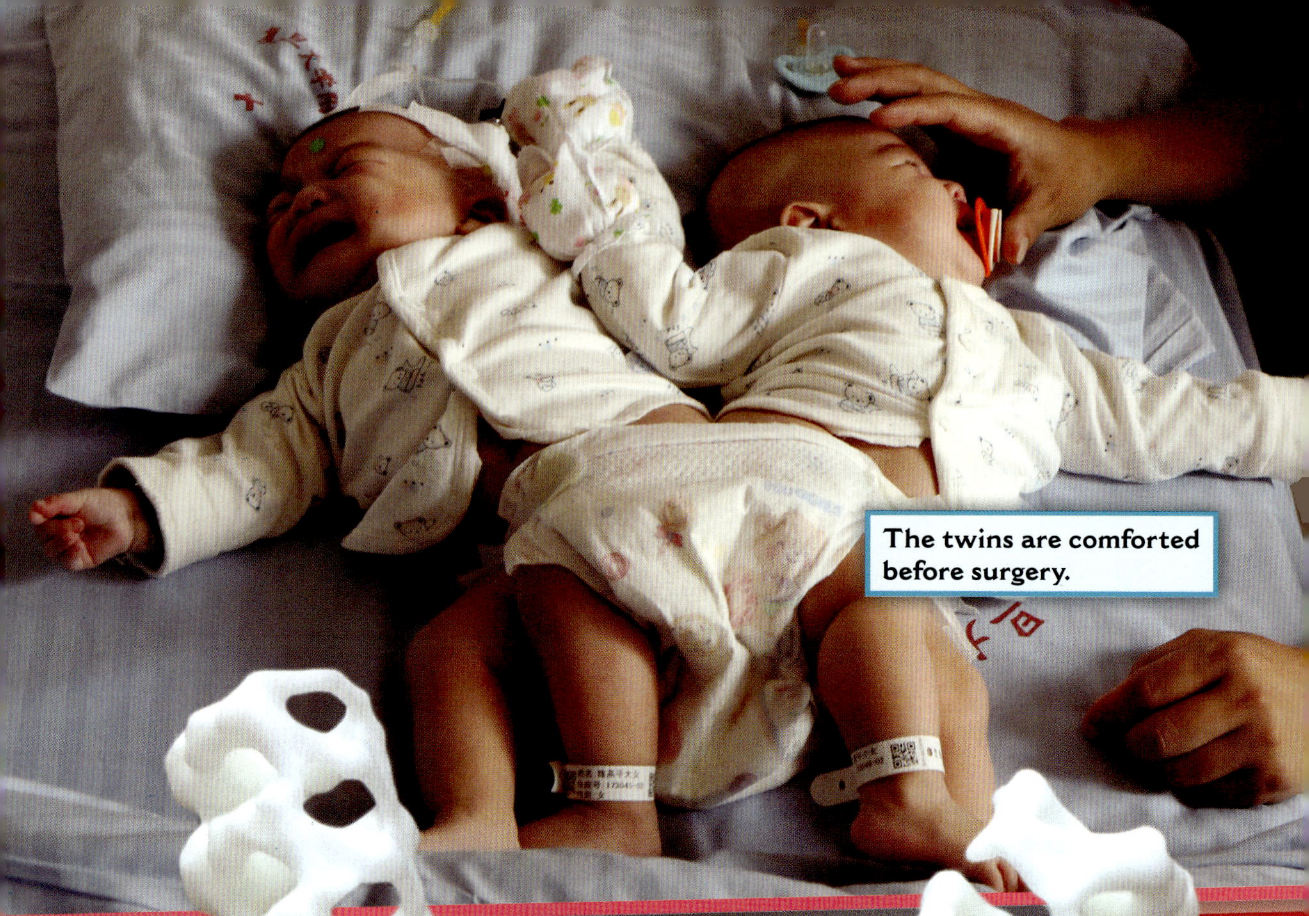

The twins are comforted before surgery.

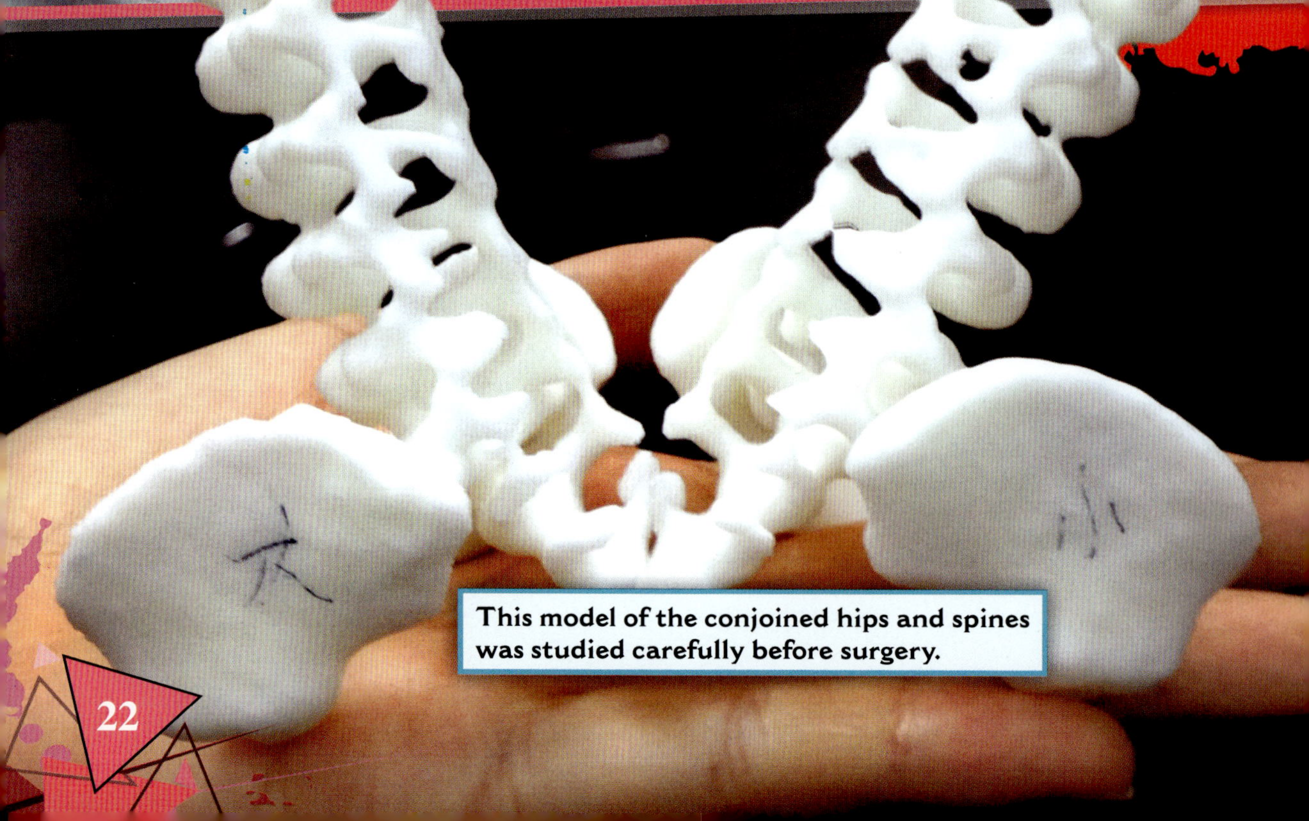

This model of the conjoined hips and spines was studied carefully before surgery.

In 2012, twin sisters were born in China. But, doctors realized that this was not an ordinary birth. The sisters were **conjoined** twins. They shared a hip and part of their spine. This is very rare.

Surgery to separate the twins would be very tough. It would also be costly. Luckily, people donated money to help pay for the surgery. And, the surgeons had a plan.

A 3-D printing company made models of the girls' conjoined body parts. Then, the surgeons practiced the surgery using the models. The models helped them improve their plan for separating the two girls. It was a big task. But, the surgeons felt they were ready. When the twins were three months old, they had the surgery. Thanks to 3-D printing, the surgery was a success! Today, both girls are living happy and healthy lives.

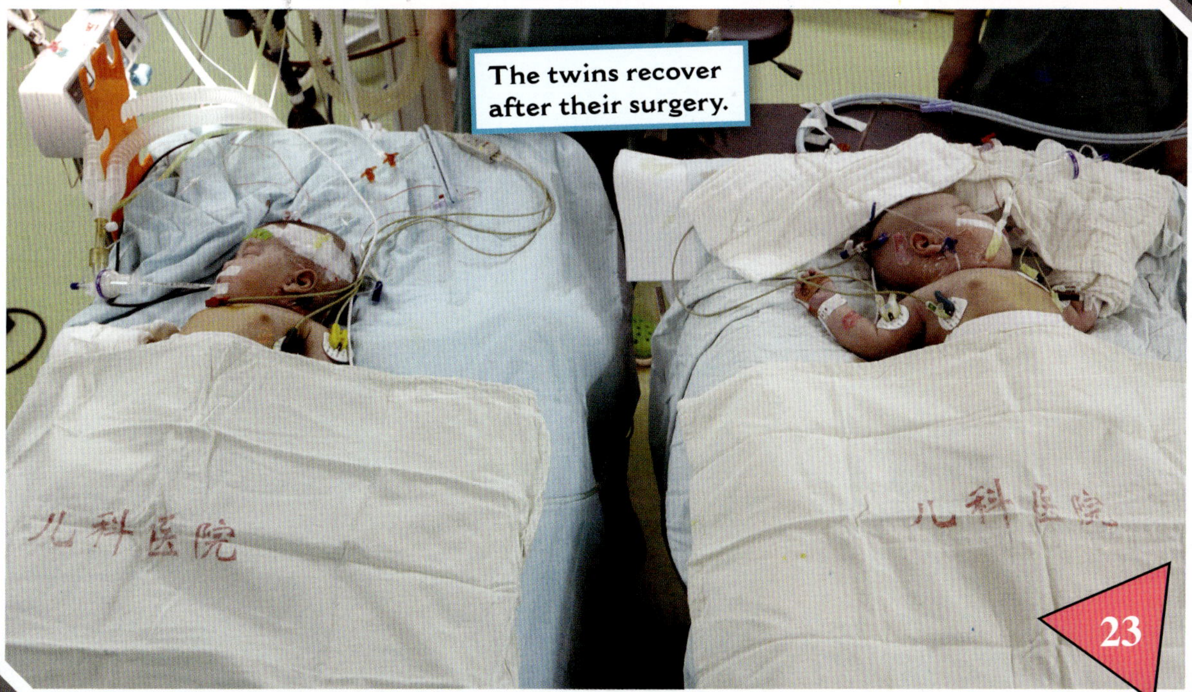

The twins recover after their surgery.

Next Steps

Scientists agree that more work needs to be done before printed organs will work inside human bodies. Blood flow is one important problem to solve. Printed organs need blood to live. They need to be attached to **blood vessels** inside the body. If scientists can find ways to make blood vessels or to make blood vessels grow, printed organs might be an option.

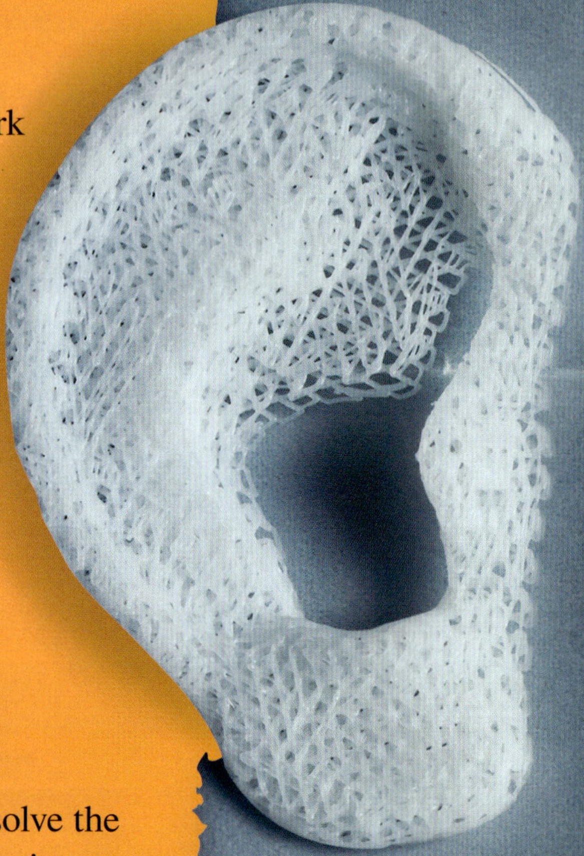

Some scientists are trying to solve the blood-flow problem. In one experiment, scientists printed a 3-D model of a human ear. It had all the bones and cells of a real ear. The scientists then attached the ear to a mouse's back. Over time, the mouse grew blood vessels that attached to the ear. After many months, the ear grew larger. This experiment showed potential that the same thing might happen in a human body.

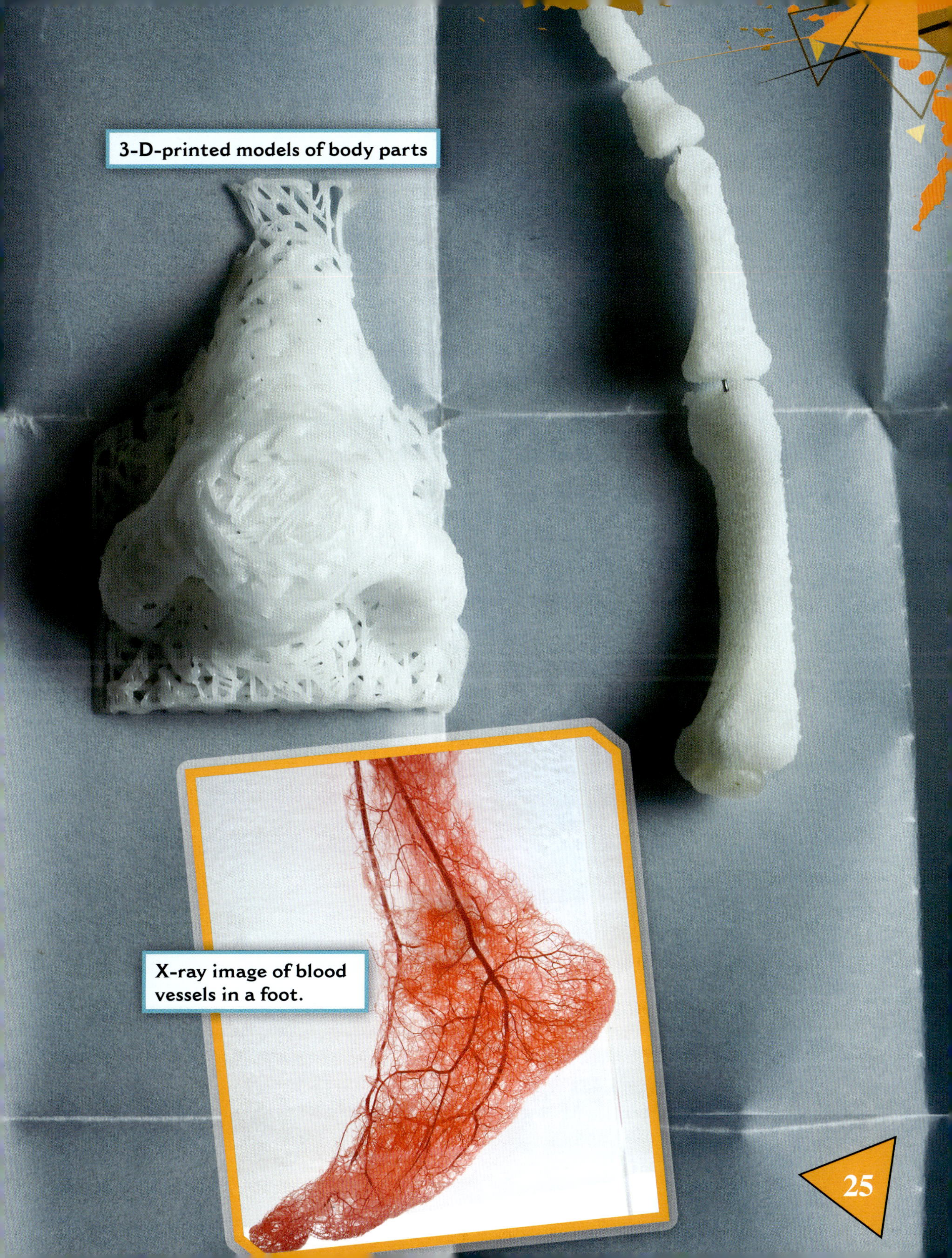

3-D-printed models of body parts

X-ray image of blood vessels in a foot.

The invention of 3-D printing is changing the way we live. Doctors and scientists are using 3-D printers to help change lives. They are able to print human body parts. Some of those body parts are made of plastic, such as prosthetic arms and legs. The same tissues and cells found in the human body are being printed in experiments. These printed body parts are helping people all over the world. From legs and fingers to ears and hearts, 3-D printing is making a difference. Now, the price of prosthetics is lower. And, people can have the surgeries they need.

The options for the future are endless. Instead of going to stores to buy things, people might print what they need right in their own homes. It is exciting to imagine the new technology that will come out next!

first car built with a 3-D-printed body

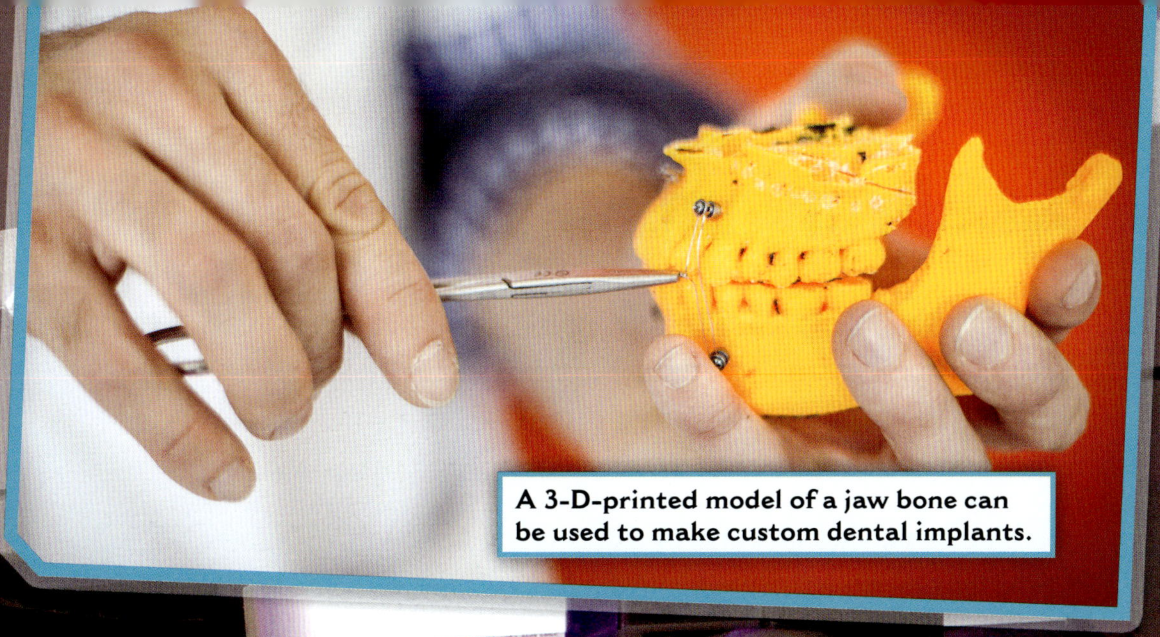

A 3-D-printed model of a jaw bone can be used to make custom dental implants.

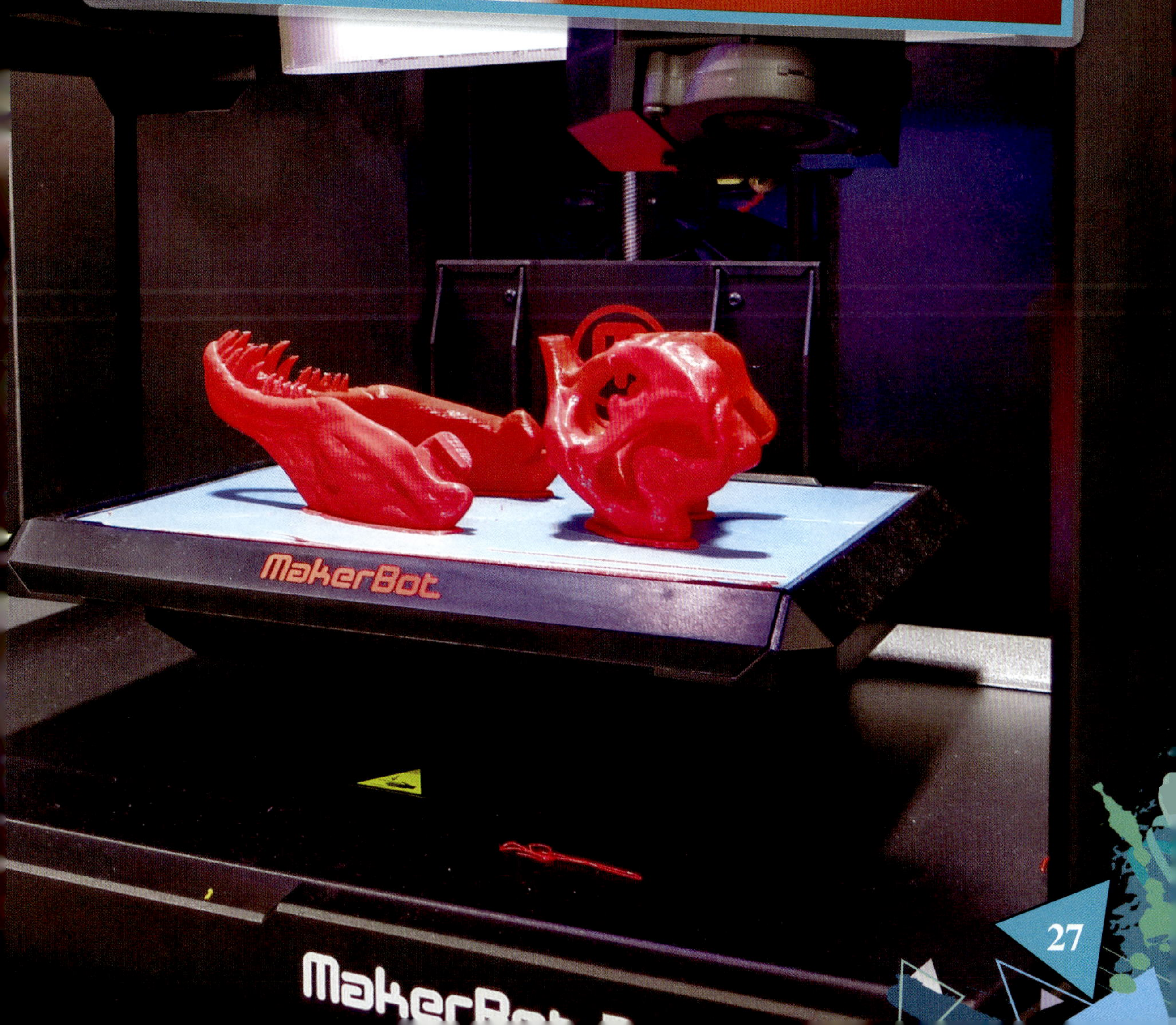

Problem Solving

The e-NABLE team is a group of volunteers who give people free prosthetic hands and arms made from 3-D printers. They have delivered thousands of printed arms and hands to adults and children all around the world.

The table shows some of the different models of hands e-NABLE prints. Imagine that 10 people are asked to choose which model they like best. The fraction of people who select each hand model is shown.

1. What fraction of people choose either Raptor Reloaded or Python?
2. What fraction of people choose Raptor, Talon, or Cyborg Beast?
3. By what fraction did more people choose Talon than Cyborg Beast?
4. Which two models combined did more than $\frac{1}{2}$ of people choose?
5. Which three models combined did less than $\frac{1}{2}$ of people choose?

Hand Model	Fraction of People
Raptor Reloaded	$\frac{3}{10}$
Raptor	$\frac{2}{10}$
Talon	$\frac{3}{10}$
Cyborg Beast	$\frac{1}{10}$
Python	$\frac{1}{10}$

Glossary

2-dimensional (2-D)—having two dimensions, such as length and width

3-dimensional (3-D)—having three dimensions, such as length, width, and depth

blood vessels—tubes that carry blood to different parts of the body

cells—the building blocks that make up all living things

conjoined—joined together

depth—the quality of how deep an object is

filament—thin, threadlike material

horizontal—lying flat; parallel to the horizon

limb—a part of a body used to move or hold something

nozzle—a hose, pipe, or tube used to control the flow of gas or liquid

organs—groups of tissues in a living organism that have a special job

plaster—a wet material that becomes hard when it dries

prosthetic—man-made part that replaces a missing or injured body part

scan—an image of a body part created by a computer

tissues—groups of cells in a living organism that work together

titanium—a strong, metallic element

transplant—transferring an organ or other body part from one individual to another

Index

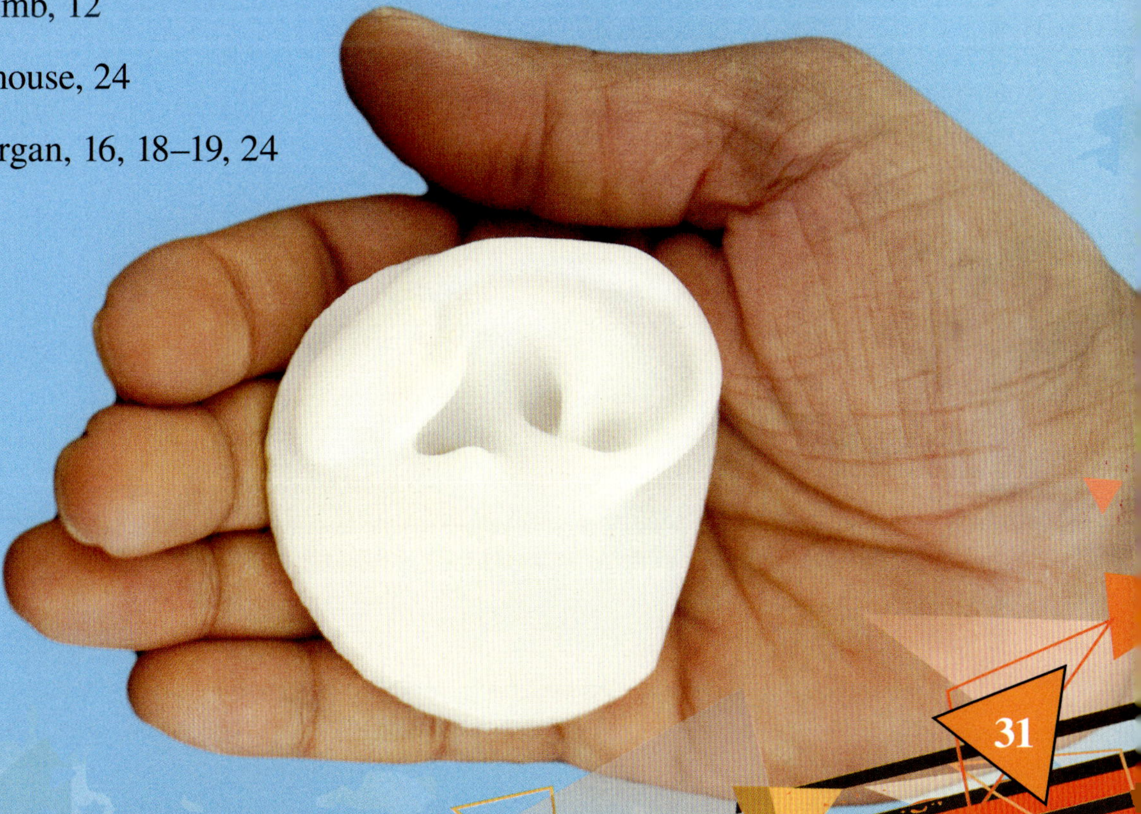

Answer Key

Let's Explore Math

page 7:

1. Models will vary. Possible model:

   $\frac{2}{6}$ $\frac{1}{6} + \frac{1}{6}$

   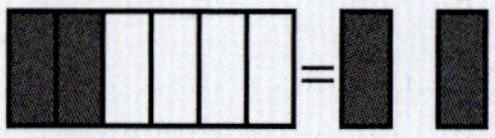

2. $\frac{2}{6} + \frac{3}{6} = \frac{5}{6}$
3. $\frac{1}{6}$; $\frac{6}{6} - \frac{5}{6} = \frac{1}{6}$

page 11:

1. Models will vary. Possible model:

   $2\frac{3}{4} = \frac{4}{4} + \frac{4}{4} + \frac{3}{4}$

2. $2\frac{3}{4} - 1\frac{1}{4} = 1\frac{2}{4}$ or $1\frac{1}{2}$

page 15:

B and D; $\frac{12}{12} - \frac{8}{12} = \frac{4}{12}$

page 17:

1. 4 millimeters; $2\frac{1}{5} + 1\frac{4}{5} = 3\frac{5}{5} = 4$
2. 2 millimeters; $6 - 4 = 2$

page 19:

C

Problem Solving

1. $\frac{4}{10}$; $\frac{3}{10} + \frac{1}{10} = \frac{4}{10}$
2. $\frac{6}{10}$; $\frac{2}{10} + \frac{3}{10} + \frac{1}{10} = \frac{6}{10}$
3. $\frac{2}{10}$; $\frac{3}{10} - \frac{1}{10} = \frac{2}{10}$
4. Raptor Reloaded and Talon; $\frac{3}{10} + \frac{3}{10} = \frac{6}{10}$; $\frac{6}{10} > \frac{1}{2}$
5. Raptor, Cyborg Beast, and Python; $\frac{2}{10} + \frac{1}{10} + \frac{1}{10} = \frac{4}{10}$; $\frac{4}{10} < \frac{1}{2}$